STORIES OF THE SIOUX

THE STORY-TELLER

STORIES OF THE SIOUX

By

CHIEF LUTHER STANDING BEAR

With Illustrations by

HERBERT MORTON STOOPS

University of Nebraska Press
Lincoln and London

First Bison Book printing: 1988
Most recent printing indicated by the first digit below:

3   4   5   6   7   8   9   10

Library of Congress Cataloging-in-Publication Data

Standing Bear, Luther, 1868?–1939.
Stories of the Sioux / by Luther Standing Bear; with
illustrations by Herbert Morton Stoops.
p.   cm.
''Bison.''
Reprint. Originally published: Boston: Houghton Mifflin, 1934.
ISBN 0-8032-4194-1.   ISBN 0-8032-9187-6 (pbk.)
1. Teton Indians—Legends. 2. Dakota Indians—Legends.
3. Indians of North America—Great Plains—Legends. I. Stoops,
Herbert Morton.   II. Title.
E99.T34S73   1988
398.2'08997—dc 19   88-12221 CIP

Reprinted by arrangement with Dolores Miller Nyerges
and Anita Miller Melbo

PREFACE

THE Sioux people have many stories which are told by the older ones in the tribe to the younger. Many main events and historical happenings of the tribe are told as stories and in this way the history of the people is recorded. These stories were not told, however, with the idea of forcing the children to learn, but for pleasure, and they were enjoyed by young and old alike. Some of these stories I have heard repeated many times. Others I have heard only once, but these I remember just as well. Perhaps it is because an Indian child is trained to use his ears carefully that his memory is so reliable.

These stories were not always told by the camp-fire during the long winter evenings, but at any time and at any place whenever and wherever the teller and the audience were in the mood. Sometimes it was Grandmother who sat on the ground, perhaps with a small stick or drawing-pencil in her hand, drawing designs on the earth as she told a story that she had known ever since she was a child herself. The children would cluster around her, either lying or squatting on the ground listening.

Sometimes Grandfather or Great-Grandfather was the story-teller as he sat and smoked at noonday. Even when on the march, if all were enjoying an afternoon rest and someone felt in the humor, a story would be related and enjoyed. So story-telling was in order with the Sioux at any and all times.

CONTENTS

I. The Old Woman who Lived with the Wolves 3

II. How the Medicine-Man Found the Lost Horses 10

III. The Arrow-Thrower 14

IV. The Hunter who was Saved by Eagles 20

V. The Deer Dreamer 26

VI. The Leap of Hawk Dreamer 28

VII. Standing Bear's Horse 32

VIII. Crow Butte 37

IX. Thunder Dreamer the Medicine-Man 41

X. Buffalo Brothers 44

XI. The Snow Woman 48

XII. The Singing Colt 51

XIII. The Woman who Killed the Owl 55

XIV. Grandmother and the Bear 58

XV. The Faithful Horse 61

XVI. The Magic Tree 65

XVII. The Year of the Buffalo 68

XVIII. The Holy Dog 71

XIX. Thunder Horse 75

XX. The First Fire 77

ILLUSTRATIONS

THE STORY-TELLER *Frontispiece*

HIS ARM ROSE HIGH FOR A DISTANCE FLIGHT 18

THE EAGLES SPREAD THEIR STRONG YOUNG WINGS 24

THE ENEMY SAW THE WHITE FIGURE OF HAWK
DREAMER FLY THROUGH THE AIR 30

THERE BELOW HIM ... STOOD A LONE BUFFALO 34

THESE WARRIORS RIDE WILDLY ABOUT ON THE
BLACK CLOUDS 42

NOT UNTIL THE FUR HOOD DROPPED ... COULD BIG
TURKEY SEE THAT HE HAD STRUCK A WOMAN 48

THE ASTONISHMENT OF THE YOUNG WARRIOR ...
TURNED TO GLADNESS 62

THE HEAD OF THIS STRANGE ANIMAL WAS NOT
SHAGGY LIKE THAT OF THE BUFFALO 72

These illustrations were made from notes supplied
in sketch form by Yellow Bird of the Oglala Sioux.

STORIES OF THE SIOUX

STORIES OF THE SIOUX

I

THE OLD WOMAN
WHO LIVED WITH THE WOLVES

THE Sioux were a people who traveled about from place to place a great deal within the borders of their own country. They did not trespass upon the territory of their neighbor Indians, but liked to make their home first here and then there upon their own ground, just as they pleased. It was not like moving from one strange town to another, but wherever they settled it was home. Taking down and putting up the tipis was not hard for them to do.

The reasons for their moving were many. Perhaps the grass for their ponies ran short, or the water in the creek became low. Maybe the game had gone elsewhere, and maybe the people just moved the camp to a fresh green spot, for the

Sioux loved pure water, pure air, and a clean place on which to put their tipis.

One day, long ago, a Sioux village was on the march. There were many people in the party, and many children. A great number of horses carried the tipis, and herds of racing and war horses were being taken care of by the young men. In this crowd was a young woman who carried with her a pet dog. The dog was young and playful, just past the puppy age. The young woman was very fond of her pet, as she had cared for it since it was a wee little thing with eyes still closed. She romped along with the pup, and the way seemed short because she played with it and with the young folks when not busy helping her mother with the packing and unpacking.

One evening Marpiyawin missed her dog. She looked and she called, but he was not to be found. Perhaps someone liked her playful pet and was keeping him concealed, but after a search she became satisfied that no one in camp was hiding him. Then she thought that perhaps he had lain down to sleep somewhere along the way and had been left behind. Then, lastly, she thought that the wolves had enticed him to join their pack. For oftentimes the Sioux dogs were coaxed away and ran with the wolf-pack, always returning, however, in a few days or weeks to the village.

So Marpiyawin, thinking the matter over, decided that she would go back over the way her people had journeyed and that somewhere she would find her dog. She would then bring him back to camp with her. Without a word to anyone, she turned back, for she had no fear of becoming lost. Nothing could befall her, so why should she fear? As she walked back, she came to the foothills at the base of the mountains where her village people had spent the summer. As she slept that night, the first snowfall of the autumn came so silently that it did not awaken her. In the morning everything was white with snow, but it was not far to the place where the village had been in camp and so determined was she to find her dog that she decided to keep going. Marpiyawin now felt that her pet had gone back to the old camping-ground, as dogs often do, and was now there howling and crying to be found.

That afternoon the snow fell thicker and faster and Marpiyawin was forced to seek shelter in a cave, which was rather dark, but warm and comfortable. She was not hungry, for in her little rawhide bag was still some *wasna*.[1] She was tired, however, so it was not long till she fell asleep, and while she slept she had a most wonderful vision. In her dream the wolves talked to her and she understood them, and when she talked to them they understood her too. They told her that she had lost her way, but that she should trust them and they would not see her suffer from cold or hunger. She replied that she would not worry, and when she awoke it was without fear, even though in the cave with her were the wolves sitting about in a friendly manner.

The blizzard raged outside for many days, still she was contented, for she was neither cold nor hungry. For meat the wolves supplied her with tender rabbits and at night they kept her body

[1] *Wasna*, meat pounded with chokecherries and pressed like head cheese. Very nourishing and easily carried.

warm with their shaggy coats of fur. As the days wore on, she and the wolves became fast friends.

But clear days finally came and the wolves offered to lead her back to her people, so they set out. They traversed many little valleys and crossed many creeks and streams; they walked up hills and down hills, and at last came to one from which she could look down upon the camp of her people. Here she must say 'Good-bye' to her friends and companions — the wolves. This made her feel very sad, though she wanted to see her people again. Marpiyawin thanked all the wolves for their kindness to her and asked what she might do for them. All they asked was that, when the long winter months came and food was scarce, she bring to the top of the hill some nice fat meat for them to eat. This she gladly promised to do and went down the hill toward the camp of her people.

As Marpiyawin neared the village, she smelled a very unpleasant odor. At first it mystified her, then she realized it was the smell of human beings. At once the knowledge came to her that the smell of humans was very different from the smell of animals. This was why she now knew that animals so readily track human beings and why the odor of man is oftentimes so offensive to them. She had been with the wolves so long that she had lost the odor of her people and now was able to see that, while man often considers the animal offensive, so do animals find man offensive.

Marpiyawin came to the camp of her people and they were happy to see her, for they had considered her lost and thought she had been taken by an enemy tribe. But she pointed to the top of the hill in the distance, and there sat her friends, their forms black against the sky. In great surprise her people looked, not knowing what to say. They thought she must have just escaped a great danger. So she explained to them that she had been lost and would have perished had not the wolves saved her life. She asked them to give her some of their fat meat that she might carry it to the top of the hill. Her people were so grateful and happy that a young man was sent about the camp telling of the safe return of Marpiyawin and collecting meat from each tipi. Marpiyawin took the meat, placed the bundle on her back, and went up the hill, while the village people looked on in wonder. When she reached the hilltop she spread the meat on the ground and the wolves ate it.

Ever after that, when the long winter months came and food was scarce and hard to find, Marpiyawin took meat to her friends the wolves. She never forgot their language and oftentimes in the winter their voices calling to her would be heard throughout the village. Then the people would ask the old woman what the wolves were saying. Their calls would be warnings that a blizzard was coming, or that the enemy was passing close, and to send out a scout or to let the old woman know that they were watching her with care.

And so Marpiyawin came to be known to the tribe as 'The Old Woman Who Lived with the Wolves,' or, in the Sioux language as, 'Win yan wan si k'ma nitu ompi ti.'

II

HOW THE MEDICINE–MAN FOUND THE LOST HORSES

ONE time the Sioux had been camped for many weeks in one place. The grass around the village was beginning to get scarce and each day the horses went farther away for food. So an order was given that the camp must move.

White Crow's horses were among the many that herded on the plains, so he set out with the rest of the braves to bring in the animals in preparation for the march. All the braves, except White Crow, returned to camp that evening, bringing their horses. White Crow's horses could not be found. But feeling confident that they were not very far away and that he would soon find them, he set out the following morning to renew his search. All day he looked, but the horses were nowhere to be found. He went far beyond the range of the rest of the herd, but his horses were not in sight. He went still farther, and searched in all the valleys and climbed many hills so that he could see great distances over the prairie. Farther and farther away he went from the village until all the canyons had been searched and all the hidden valleys had been explored. But White Crow's horses had disappeared as completely as if an enemy had stolen them, yet no enemy had been reported. White Crow knew all the land of the Sioux, so he grew more puzzled each day as the search went on. At last he decided to return home.

When White Crow reached the village, he built a small frame lodge of willows. This he covered with heavy buffalo-robes. Then he covered the floor of the room with branches of the sweet-smelling and healing sagebrush. In the center was left a small space, slightly hollowed out, where hot stones would be placed, for this was to be a sweat-lodge. Outside, and not far from the door, White Crow prepared a fire of cottonwood bark in which he placed smooth stones to heat.

He then gave his daughter the sacred pipe and
sent her to the tipi of the medicine-man. The
medicine-man accepted the pipe by smoking it,
and at once went to the lodge which White Crow
had built. Disrobing, he went into the lodge,
taking with him his medicine and a whistle made
from a wing-bone of an eagle. White Crow took
in the hot stones and poured water upon them,
making a heavy steam that filled the lodge. While
the medicine-man was enduring the purifying
sweat, he sang his sacred songs and played soft
tunes upon his whistle.

When he had finished, he asked that the blanket
which covered the entrance to the sweat-lodge
be removed and the stones allowed to cool. Then
he dried his body with the leaves of the sage.
When he came from the lodge he was again handed
the pipe. He performed the sacred ceremony
and smoked the pipe in silence. When the last
puff of smoke had floated away, the medicine-
man said: 'White Crow, I have seen your horses.
Go north for one camping distance. Climb the
hill that you will then see in front of you. At the

foot of the hill on the other side is a meadow. There are your horses.'

The medicine-man then put his whistle and medicine in his deerskin bag and went away.

White Crow started in the direction the medicine-man told him to go. He found the hill and climbed it, and there on the other side in the meadow were his five horses. He drove them home, and one of the best he gave to the medicine-man.

III

THE ARROW–THROWER

TURNING BEAR was the famous arrow-thrower of the Sioux. There were braves who were famous for throwing the ball, and there were those who could shoot the arrow farther than any other man; but Turning Bear could throw the arrow so far that no one had ever been able to beat him.

Turning Bear was a tall, straight fellow who had lived all his life either riding his pony or engaging with the other boys of the village in the strenuous games which Indian boys play. In the winter time he played *pte-he-ste*, which is a throwing game, and his arm became strong and powerful. As well as being a good arrow-thrower, Turning Bear had also become a fine huntsman, and ever since he had been twelve years of age had always gone with the men on their buffalo hunts.

One morning in early spring the scouts reported

a herd of buffalo near. The supply of meat, after the long winter, was low, so all the warriors prepared for the hunt. All were eager to go, so that when the party left for the chase not a man was left in the village. Only the women and children remained to make preparations for taking care of the meat that the men would bring home and to tan the skins. So everybody in the village was busy too.

It was a great and successful hunt. Every warrior got a buffalo, and some of them got more. When the herd had scattered over the plain and disappeared, then every man got busy skinning the animals and getting the meat ready to load on the pack-ponies for the ride home. It would be late before the hunters would get back to the village with their laden ponies, but just the same everyone was happy.

Turning Bear was one of the lucky huntsmen. He had skinned his buffalo and had packed the meat and hide on his pony, and was ready to turn homeward the first of all. He would reach the village before the rest of the warriors, so he meant to tell the women the good news of the hunt and to ask them to prepare a good feast.

As he hurried on his way he felt very satisfied with the day. There would be plenty of meat in camp for a long while, and there would be many skins for the women to tan for moccasins and for repairing the worn-out tipis.

Looking over his weapons as he walked along, he remembered that he had broken his bow-string early in the chase, and had restrung his bow with the extra string which all good and careful hunters carry. But this, too, had broken, and his bow was useless. But this caused him no worry, for there was nothing to fear, and he thought that when evening came, after a hearty supper of fresh buffalo meat he and the rest of the warriors would fix up broken bows, re-feather arrows, and make new sinew strings.

Turning Bear was happy and contented. It was not long before he could see the green trees of the stream beside which was the village. The afternoon had been warm, and when Turning Bear came to the creek he let his pony walk in the paths that were shaded. All was so peaceful and quiet. Here and there were little green meadows which looked so fresh after being covered with snow all winter, and the leaves of the cottonwood and willow trees glistened with every little breeze. Turning Bear was a trained man and not a sight or sound was missed by him.

In one of the little green spots Turning Bear saw several horses grazing. One was his father's favorite horse and a runner. Turning Bear watching the splendid animal, saw him raise his head and look intently at some object which Turning Bear could not see. The animal kept up his head and thrust his ears forward. The other horses then did likewise. Turning Bear understood 'horse language.' He knew that no Sioux, not even a woman or a child from the village, was hidden in the thick willow growth. It was, of course, some prowling animal, and the horses had plainly showed that they did not like its presence.

As Turning Bear felt for his bow, a man came from the thicket of willows. His face was painted red, and he carried a bow and quiver full of arrows. An enemy! How many more were hidden in the shadows, it was impossible to tell. The village was unprotected, and not a hunter had yet come with his meat. Turning Bear was alone and did not even have a weapon. He felt helpless.

It was clear what the enemy was seeking. He was trying to rope a horse and of course had selected the finest. His father's horse! He must do something! But the enemy might number many and he was alone and unarmed.

Turning Bear again felt of his arrows. Only three remained. But without more thought of the enemy that might be hidden, Turning Bear took an arrow from his quiver and his arm rose high for a distance flight. It sped swift and true. It came close to the body of the man and disappeared in the brush. His second arrow followed so close that it might have been shot by another warrior. This arrow found its mark in the shoulder of the enemy now flying for the cover of brush and willows. Still for flight, Turn-

HIS ARM ROSE HIGH FOR A DISTANCE FLIGHT

ing Bear held his third and last arrow for the foe that might now swarm from the woods.

But all was quiet and Turning Bear went on to the village. When the warriors came in from the hunt, the scouts were sent out and came back with the broken arrow. The blood of the enemy had left its trail. He had been alone and had run away, thinking, no doubt, that he had been attacked by the returning hunters.

That night around the camp-fire praises were sung for the bravery of Turning Bear the Arrow-Thrower.

IV

THE HUNTER WHO WAS
SAVED BY EAGLES

WHEN I was a boy Grandfather told this story to me, and he said he knew the hunter.

Sioux hunters are very brave. They must be as brave as a warrior, but, besides this, they must be wise to the ways of animals and birds.

This hunter whom my Grandfather knew was very wise. He could track any kind of animal whose footprint he saw on the ground. Furthermore, he could see tracks on rain-washed earth or among rocks that other hunters would not see. By these footprints he could tell whether the animal that made them was walking or running, or whether it was jumping and leaping as it sped over the ground. This wise hunter could even tell what sort of enemy was pursuing the fleeing animal. So long had he been out in the solitudes of nature breathing only pure air and drinking only pure water that he could smell the various animals when they came close to him just as the animals could smell him.

When he came to a deer trail the hunter could tell how long since the deer had traveled the path. If the tracks were far apart, the animal had been walking fast and would now be far from him, but if the tracks were close together, the animal had been traveling slowly and was probably not far away.

Even the tangled chokecherry thickets could not keep things hidden from him. He could tell whether the bears had feasted yesterday or to-day. He could tell just where they had lain down to rest or sleep and in what direction they had gone. All the secrets of the 'forest people' were his. The woods and the plains were like a book that he read each day and that told him of the travels and lives of his brothers the animals.

One day this hunter was a long way from his village. He had killed a buffalo and had loaded the meat on his pony. While traveling

toward home, he noticed two eagles circling high
about a cliff. Not being in a hurry to reach home
he stopped to watch them. Finally he decided
to climb to the top of the cliff better to observe
their flight. There he saw the two eagles were
keeping watch over a nest which had been built
on a ledge far below the top of the cliff. He tied
his pony to a tree, and, lying down, peered over
at the nest. In it were two young eagles; they
were about half-grown and fully feathered. To
a hunter here was temptation. So he took the meat
off his horse and got the skin which was wrapped
about it. This he cut into strips for a rope. The
hide being fresh, he cut it into wide strips to give
it the strength of a dried rope. One end he tied
to a pine tree that grew not far from the edge of
the cliff, and the other end he tied around his
waist. Looping the rest of the rope in his hand,
he slowly went over the edge of the cliff. This
was thrilling sport and delighted this brave hunter.
He was thinking how fortunate **he was** to have
noticed the two old eagles flying in the sky. But
his pleasant thoughts were interrupted, for the

skin, being raw, stretched too thin and it came apart, letting him drop to the ledge. He looked up to see the end of the rope hanging beyond his reach, while below him lay the rocky bottom of the cliff to which he could not leap. He expected to see the old eagles swoop down upon him and to see the young ones attempt to fly away. Being a wise hunter, he sat very still, glad that the young eagles did not fly away, for that reassured the old eagles which continued to circle above his head. Nothing happened to him, so he began to think. Up above was his horse, which would stand patiently waiting for him to return. The fine meat lying there would spoil, and he, forced to stay on the ledge, would starve to death. He tried to think of some means of getting away, but no thought came to him. He tried shouting at the top of his voice, but no one heard, and his calls passed away into the air like smoke. The parent eagles continued to circle close, so he knew that no one was near. Every now and then his mind would go back to his pony waiting for him up on the edge of the cliff, and he thought how comfortable it would be were he once more riding on its back.

At last he decided on a plan and made up his mind to carry it out, for to remain on the ledge meant death to him anyway. So carefully and quietly he began to creep toward the young eagles in the nest. They did not take fright, so slow and noiseless was he. He knew that if he snatched at them roughly, they would tussle in his grasp and perhaps he would not capture them. But he knew the ways of eagles, so did not frighten them. When close enough to touch both eagles, he removed the rope from around his waist. This he cut into two pieces. In a moment he had secured both birds by their feet. One of them he tied to his left wrist, the other he tied to his right wrist. He stretched out his arms, and the young eagles, too perplexed to flutter, sat motionless upon his wrists. He walked to the edge of the ledge and for a moment balanced. With a prayer to the Great Mystery he leaped. The eagles spread their strong young wings and like an eagle himself he landed at the bottom of the cliff safe and sound.

THE EAGLES SPREAD THEIR STRONG YOUNG WINGS

Reaching his horse, and with his meat loaded, the hunter started happily on his way home. He took the young eagles with him and fed and watered them. Then he painted their heads and necks red, and carried them back to the edge of the cliff. On a nice white deerskin he reverently placed them and left them there in thankfulness to the Great Mystery and Keeper of All Things.

V

THE DEER DREAMER

THERE is a place famous to all the Sioux called the Deer Run. It was to this place that the Deer Dreamer with his mysterious powers and medicine sent the deer when meat and skins grew scarce in camp. There the hunters could easily kill all that were needed for meat and skins.

The Deer Run was an unwooded space on the bank of a river. This bank was high and steep, and at its foot the river ran dark and deep. No deer would leap from this bank. A narrow path was cleared through the woods up to the space on the bank of the river. On either side of the path the woods were thick, and the limbs and boughs had been laced and interlaced to form an unbreakable fence through which the deer could not go. This left but one entrance to the deer enclosure. The day before the deer were to be run into the Deer Run, the Deer Dreamer purified himself in the sweat-lodge. He then asked the Great Mystery to send the deer to the people, as they were in need of meat and clothing.

Early in the morning the Deer Dreamer sent out two scouts, each carrying the magic medicine. The scouts walked in a great circle and all the deer within this circle were driven toward the path which led to the enclosure. If a deer approached the footprints made by the scout, it would not be able to cross and get outside of the circle on account of the magic medicine. So steadily and slowly the deer moved toward the run.

Soon a herd of deer would be within the enclosure, so the warriors would have a great hunt, and take home much meat, and many skins to be tanned for garments.

VI

THE LEAP OF HAWK DREAMER

Even in the days after the Sioux had horses, they still liked to hunt and travel on foot. They were so strong and swift themselves that they did not depend greatly on horses to carry them about. They could run fast over the hills and go long distances in a day. They could climb mountains and steep crags so that they could see far out over the country. Silently and quickly they could creep through the dense undergrowth of the river-bottoms, and when ready for the buffalo hunt could get very close by creeping in the tall grass.

When on the warpath the Sioux could hide themselves behind rocks and trees better if not on horseback. So they were very self-reliant, and their strong arms and legs were their weapons.

Hawk Dreamer was a very brave hunter, and could run very fast and endure long trips. Also he was a famous scout. He had fasted in the solitudes of the mountains for the purpose of gaining magic power, and the Hawk had come to him with many secrets, so when he awoke from his dream he became known as Hawk Dreamer. Thereafter he became swift as a Hawk and feared nothing from any foe.

One day Hawk Dreamer went out to look over the hunting-ground of the Sioux, and, should he find the enemy on the land of his tribe, to drive them away. With him were several scouts and warriors. In a day or so they sighted the enemy, and Hawk Dreamer went alone to see how many were in the party and what they were doing. When scouting, he dressed in white, and though very skillful, he was discovered. He at once started back for his warriors.

Hawk Dreamer leaped from rock to rock like a swift-footed deer. He went over creeks and streams like a bird. Though he disappeared from the enemy over a hill, when he reached the bottom the enemy had followed to the top. So on the chase went. The enemy warriors were swift and strong, too, and there being many of them, they closed on him on both sides. Straight ahead he must go. To the right was the enemy and to the left was the enemy. Still he did not fear. So long as he could run he was safe. He was in the land of the Sioux and felt that the swiftness of his friend the Hawk was with him.

Ahead of Hawk Dreamer lay a stream, once across which he would be safe, no matter how many the enemy numbered. The bed of the stream lay deep in a steep and rocky chasm. But there was a way down to the bottom of the stream over a rough trail like a stairway, with holes in the rocks for footholds. When he reached the edge of the stream, with the thick brush hiding him, he would disappear down this stairway as if he had leaped into the river.

But the enemy was closer now, and so fast did Hawk Dreamer go that his white-robed body seemed to skim over the brush-tops. To the left of him the enemy was now so close that they had begun to laugh and shout at him, hoping to unnerve him, as was the custom of the Plains

THE ENEMY SAW THE WHITE FIGURE OF HAWK DREAMER FLY
THROUGH THE AIR

Indians. Then Hawk Dreamer realized that the enemy had blocked the stairway. He could turn neither to the right nor to the left. Straight ahead he must go, though every minute his pursuers were nearer. No man and no pony had ever crossed this awful space. Even his friends on the other side could not help him now.

But Hawk Dreamer had no thought of surrender. No Sioux ever surrendered! So he cried out: 'Hawk, give me power! Give me power! Oh, Brother Hawk, give me the strength and swiftness of your wings!'

He put his faith in the Hawk, and as he did so felt his strength grow and his body became lighter. Only his toes touched the ground.

Again he prayed: 'Brother Hawk, oh, Brother Hawk, give me of your power! I have never killed a hawk and I shall always spare your lives! Help me, Brother Hawk!' Then he leaped.

When the enemy saw the white figure of Hawk Dreamer fly through the air like a bird and land safely on the bare edge of the other side of the terrible space, they stood as men turned to stone.

Hawk Dreamer was saved.

VII

STANDING BEAR'S HORSE

For a long time the enemies of the Sioux had been troubling them, taking their ponies and running off the buffalo. At length Standing Bear the First asked the braves to go with him to help punish the enemy and to make them return to their own land. Ten warriors responded, so the party left for the warpath. All traveled on foot except Standing Bear. He rode his horse, a beautiful and intelligent animal. Standing Bear thought more of this trustworthy friend than of any of his other possessions. For days the party traveled toward the edge of their land, the enemy always keeping out of sight, for they wanted no open fights with the Sioux, who they knew were the bravest of brave fighters.

At last the Sioux met the enemy and gave them punishment they were to remember for some time. But by this time they were at the farthest point of their homeland and it was a long journey home, so Standing Bear and his warriors were very glad to turn back toward their village.

Great plains lay between them and their tipis on the bank of Porcupine Creek. Coming away from their village they had traveled over beautiful plains which were soft with waving grasses and plentiful with animals that fed here and there. But on their return they discovered that a fire had swept the plain and everywhere it was black with ashes. There was not a sign of life. The animals had fled in front of the heat and smoke of the prairie fire. For days they traveled, but no buffalo were in sight, and even the birds, always so many, were not to be seen or heard. Fields of sunflowers lay on the ground, their stalks dead and black. The little streams were edged with grass and weeds trying to grow once more.

As the days wore on, the food that the warriors carried ran low, and only in small spaces, far apart, could the trustful pony find a few mouthfuls to eat. All of the travelers became hungry and weary. Day after day they hoped to find a stray animal, but the land was deserted of all creatures. At night the warriors lay down exhausted, hoping that the next day their luck would be better. Standing Bear's horse seemed to sense the misery of the braves, and the helplessness of his own want and hunger. When they lay asleep at night, he acted as scout. At the slightest noise he would arouse them with a snort, and they would awake, fearing a chance enemy or hoping for an animal at which to shoot. The horse was their most dependable friend, and as they grew weaker they watched him closer for warnings.

At last, however, the warriors became so weak they could no longer make a day's journey. Without food they would never reach their village; so they begged Standing Bear to kill his horse that they might continue the journey. Standing Bear looked at his suffering friends with pity. He was weak and hungry himself, yet when he looked at his faithful horse, his heart was touched. It was hard to see his friends starving, but when he again looked at his pony standing dejectedly

THERE BELOW HIM... STOOD A LONE BUFFALO

but submissively by, he knew it would be hard to sacrifice a friend.

Turning to his warriors, he said: 'Wait for one more day. If tomorrow we do not find food, then I shall kill my horse to save your lives.'

The next morning the warriors sat on the ground. They could not go on without food. Standing Bear mounted his horse and rode away. He wanted to go away alone and pray to the Great Mystery — pray for food that his companions and his pony might be spared. Slowly he and the pony went to the top of a hill. With eyes closed, Standing Bear prayed. When he opened them, the miracle had happened. There below him in a little patch of green by a seeping spring stood a lone buffalo! The pony seemed to know the thought of his master. He ran as fast as he could — ran as if he knew he was running to save men's lives and his own.

Standing Bear wasted not a shot. The first one weakened his game. The second one — and his prayer was answered. He rode back to the top of the hill and waved his blanket three times;

then he began the skinning. In later years Standing Bear the First showed Standing Bear the Second the exact spot where the Great Mystery had placed the buffalo.

VIII

CROW BUTTE

IN southeastern Dakota a long low line of hills runs out into the prairie as if it were going to level out and disappear into the plain, when suddenly it rises into a high rocky butte that can be seen for many miles around. So high and straight is this butte that it has long been a landmark for the Sioux. Later, when the white man came to the country, they used it for a landmark also. Standing straight and alone, one is reminded of a scout on the lookout for an enemy, or a soldier on guard.

The face of this butte is a sheer wall almost as smooth as a man's hand. Nothing grows on it. The smoothness of the stone wall is broken by a split from bottom to top, but that is all.

Though it stands in silence, this lone mountain speaks to the Indian, for it has watched the Sioux tribes pass back and forth before it for centuries.

At the opposite end from its stone face the bluff lowers slightly and joins the hills, but it is still steep and rocky, and there is only one path by which its top may be reached. This trail is rough and winding, and it takes a strong warrior to climb to the little plateau at the top. It is narrow, and only one man can travel it at a time. An army or a war-party would have to go up single-file. A pony could follow the trail only a short distance; it could never reach the top.

The level top of the bluff is covered with boulders, and a few pines grow here and there. White River runs not far from the foot of this bluff, and in summer the Sioux often camped in the timber which bordered the stream. Always this place, high in the air, had an attraction for the small boys of the camp, so one day we rode our ponies over and started up the steep path. Though the ponies were hardy and well trained, and the boys good riders, the animals were soon left by the path and the rest of the way was made on foot.

This is the story that the old folks told us younger ones in response to our questions.

One time a band of Crows came into the land of the Sioux, looking for a chance to steal some horses. As soon as the Crows were discovered, the Sioux gave chase. The Crows were unable to get away by running back the way they had come, and found themselves up against the bluff. With only one direction in which to run, they took to the steep path that led to the top of the butte. It was not a matter of choice with them, but their only means of escape. All along the way they abandoned their ponies, but managed to save themselves. At the end of the chase the Crows had all reached the top of the bluff, but the Sioux did not follow them, for it was late in the day. Guarding the path, the Sioux made camp, laughing and joking at the discomfort of the Crows up on top of the butte. The Sioux warriors gathered about their camp-fires enjoying their meal, and went to bed feeling that their enemy was securely imprisoned. High on top of the bluff, on its plateau, could be seen the glare of the Crow fires. All night they burned, lighting up the sky.

When morning came, no haste was made to attack the Crows. And not until some keen-eyed warrior saw footprints at the foot of the bluff were the Sioux aroused. Looking up, they saw, some fifty feet above, the end of a horse-hide rope, fresh and raw, swinging loose in the breeze. Sioux warriors climbed the path with all haste. When they reached the top of the bluff, the story was pictured there. One horse by some manner or means had reached the top with the Crows. It had been killed and skinned, and the hide used to lengthen the rawhide rope which some Crow warrior had. Around the stump of a pine tree the rope was secured, and down that, one by one, the Crow warriors had slid as far as they could go. Then they jumped and swam the river. It was a dangerous escape, and even the brave Sioux were amazed.

Since that time both Indians and white men have called this place Crow Butte. In the name is the story of the famous escape retained in the memory of the people.

IX

THUNDER DREAMER
THE MEDICINE-MAN

THAT our medicine-men had great powers we never doubted. But even so, sometimes they performed strange things that filled us with wonder. We knew that they were close to the source of all things — Mother Nature, or the Mother of All Things — Earth — and that from her were learned many things that only medicine-men could know.

One day several bands of Sioux had come together for feasting and dancing. There were thousands of Indians in the gathering, and their tipis spread out into a very large village. The braves had decorated themselves and were eager to dance in their fine feathers so that the maidens would all watch and admire them.

The sky was clear and beautiful, the breezes soft and gentle, so that the smoke from the tipis floated gently away and the feathers of the braves fluttered gracefully as they walked about or rode on their prancing ponies.

Suddenly out of the sky an angry little breeze rushed through the village and stirred up the dust. Everyone was gay, however, and paid no attention to it. In a short time the Wind spoke again, and as the Indians understand the voice of the Wind, they knew he was a messenger of Storm; but still the sky was so soft and blue that they did not heed him. When the Wind spoke the third time, it was with a louder and angrier voice, and a black Cloud showed his face through the treetops. Then the village people looked up and wondered why the Sky People were displeased. Hidden by the black Clouds, the noise of the Thunder Warriors riding wildly on their horses could be heard. The Wind swept more strongly between the tipis and jerked at flying feathers more rudely. Then Rain came, and big drops splashed down on the painted robes of the girls and the finery of the braves. Women ran to their tipis and began staking them tight, so that the Wind would not tear them down. Children scur-

THESE WARRIORS RIDE WILDLY ABOUT ON THE BLACK CLOUDS

ried to their mothers. Everyone ran to shelter.

Undisturbed by the excitement, Thunder Dreamer the medicine-man walked to the center of the circle of tipis. He was stripped to the waist and carried a deer-hoof rattle. His hair was without a feather or decoration, and hung straight and plain down his back. Thunder Dreamer called to the people to gather around him and stand silently and with faith. Then he sang his Thunder song. As the people watched, their faith grew. Thunder Dreamer raised his face to the sky and his voice seemed to reach beyond the Clouds. The Wind began to quiet and Rain gradually ceased. When he finished his song, he raised his arms and gave silent command for the Clouds to part. The Clouds divided, and when the Sun was again shining the people went on with their preparations for the feast.

Such was the power of Thunder Dreamer.

X

BUFFALO BROTHERS

AT ONE time great fields of the golden sunflower grew on the plains of the Sioux country. Both the Sioux and the buffalo loved this beautiful flower. Its leaves were so bright and green, and the yellow petals more lovely and delicate than gold.

Many little yellow birds, so many they could not be counted, hovered over the fields of sunflowers. They loved the sunflower, too, and their feathers were almost as yellow as the petals arranged so neatly around the centers of brown. The birds picked at these brown seeds and talked a lot while they were about it. No wonder, then, that we boys liked to lie around on pleasant days in these fields and take in all the sights and sounds. Everything interested us.

The buffalo liked to wallow their big heads in the sunflowers, and many times we saw them with long stems wound about the left horn, for they never wore them on the right horn. Perhaps they did this to decorate themselves, or maybe they liked the smell of the flowers. We only knew that they liked the sunflower.

Of course, we boys did not try to get very close to the buffalo, but we sat on our ponies at a distance and watched them. In the summer, if the flies were bad, the buffalo raised the dust with their horns and the dust-clouds would hide them from us for a while. Sometimes we saw them play, and sometimes we saw them swim in a lake with only their big black heads above the water. From a distance it looked like a single moving black body on the surface of the water.

One day a great hunt took place. The braves killed many buffalo and brought home many hides.

The next day some of us boys rode out on the prairie. No buffalo were in sight. Everything was quiet except the birds in the sunflower fields. I rode alone up a little hill, and, looking over, saw two buffalo. I was surprised, for I thought that they had all been killed or had been frightened away. I sat on my pony and watched. One buffalo was on the ground, his feet under him; the other was nosing and pushing the fallen one about with his head and horns. I was curious, and watched for several moments before I realized that the buffalo on the ground was either ill or wounded. The day before, no doubt, he had been wounded, but had been able to escape the hunters. At this spot he had lain down weak from the loss of blood. With the grunted urges of the helpful buffalo, the wounded one would try to rise. Each time he tried, he got upon his forefeet, but each time sank back again. However, this seemed to be satisfactory, for the friendly buffalo moved on.

The next day my curiosity brought me back to the place, but I came alone. The wounded buffalo still sat on the ground. After I had waited for an hour or so, I saw the other buffalo coming. When he got to the wounded one, there was a greeting with horns and head. The well buffalo encouraged the sick one with rubbing and poking, and pushing him with his head. The poor fellow rose to his feet and stood for a moment, but sank back to the ground again. The second time he got to his feet he walked for a few steps and again lay down. But he was in a clean place and there was some green grass close by. In a little while the visiting buffalo went back to his herd somewhere in the distance and out of sight.

I could not now help going back to see what was to happen, so the next day I was looking on again. The unfailing friend came as before, and the stricken buffalo must have revived considerably, for after some coaxing he arose on weakened legs, but followed his friend away at a slow but steady pace.

I saw them disappear, and I went home feeling that I had been made better by this lesson in kindness.

XI

THE SNOW WOMAN

SOMETIMES the Sioux villages were far apart, yet it is necessary for them to communicate with one another. Important messages must sometimes be taken from one band to the other. In the summer-time traveling was pleasant, but in winter, when the paths and trails were blocked with snow and the animals became hungry, it took a brave man to be a news carrier.

The news carrier was usually a brave who was both young and strong, and did not mind the snow and cold. He was sure to be welcomed in every village, and was feasted, entertained, and anxiously listened to as he told the stories gathered on his journey from village to village. He was often given so much dried meat that he could not eat it all, so he carried a long pointed stick on which he strung the dried meat that had been presented to him. Sometimes he arrived home with two or three long sticks of dried meat.

NOT UNTIL THE FUR HOOD DROPPED... COULD BIG TURKEY SEE
THAT HE HAD STRUCK A WOMAN

One time, at the end of a long winter day, Big Turkey, a news carrier, stopped for an evening meal. He staked out his pony and cleared a place for a fire. Everything was snow-covered, but he took a stick and struck the logs which lay on the ground, and the snow fell off; he then rolled them to the fire. Sitting near the blaze he dried his moccasins and ate the dried meat and *wasna* which he carried in his deerskin bag. He was pleased with his journey, for he had had a good time. There had been singing and feasting for him, and he had been asked to tell over and over again the happenings of his travels and the news from other villages. He had enjoyed all this and had gathered more news to carry on to the next village.

The evening grew darker, and Big Turkey looked about for some more logs to keep the fire going throughout the night. One log looked as if a good size to roll to the fire, so he struck it a sharp blow with the stick. Big Turkey was a brave man, but when the log which he struck sprang up with a piercing scream, he was too scared to move. The snow spattered in all directions as the log bounded up and a human being wrapped in a buffalo-robe rose before him. Filled with fright, the two people looked at each other. Not until the fur hood dropped from the head of the figure could Big Turkey see that he had struck a woman. In the darkness they stood and looked each other over. Then the woman laughed; it was Star Woman.

When Big Turkey and Star Woman sat by the fire they told each other why they were there. Star Woman had run away from her village. Her brother had made arrangements for her marriage to a man whom she did not love. The man had brought many horses to her brother, and he had been tempted with the sight of riches; so he told Star Woman to prepare for marriage. This she would not do, so she had run away. She had walked many miles and had lain down to rest. Her buffalo blanket had kept her warm as the snow gently fell and covered her.

Big Turkey took her with him to the next village, and there the marriage feast of Big Turkey and Star Woman was celebrated.

XII

THE SINGING COLT

THE camp of the Sioux had moved from the place where they had spent the winter to a new place where the grass was green and plentiful. The women were putting up the tipis and bringing in firewood. The children were helping their mothers, and the men were taking care of the ponies.

White Feather, the Horse Dreamer, was searching for his otter-skin quiver. Of all his belongings his otter-skin quiver was the one he prized the most. Whenever he wore it at the big feasts and ceremonies, he was envied by all the other young braves. But somewhere along the trail it had been lost, so he must go back and find it.

Now, the horse was the guiding friend and spirit of the Horse Dreamer, and stood ready at all times to give of his strength and goodness whenever the Dreamer was in need of help. White Feather, being a Horse Dreamer, never rode a horse, but always traveled on foot.

He had arrived at a place about midway between the old camping-place and the new one. The trail ran close to the banks of a river. He could not see very far ahead, for the trees and the blackberry and wild-rose bushes grew thick along the way. Walking along and wondering where he would find his lovely quiver, White Feather was surprised to hear a voice singing. It was not a song of gladness, but of sadness. A sobbing voice sang: 'I am all alone. I have lost my mother and the way is hard for me.' White Feather's heart was touched, so he hastened his steps to help the person in distress. The voice came near, and here in the path coming toward him was a poor little tired pony, his head hanging low in sorrow. It was a pretty little fellow with white spots on his forehead and two dainty white forefeet. White Feather could not help liking the helpless little colt, and, seeing that he was grief-stricken, talked kindly to him.

The Sioux some weeks before had captured a band of wild horses. Among them was the mother of Singing Colt. She had been brought in, tied to the neck of a tame horse, with Singing Colt following at her heels. But for some reason she had become sick and died, leaving Singing Colt alone. When the camp moved, the colt had tried to follow, but, growing tired, stopped by the trail to rest. He had fallen asleep, and when he awoke the camp was gone. So he was traveling alone, where, he did not know.

White Feather prepared to take Singing Colt back with him to camp where he would have plenty of food and would grow strong. As they turned to go, there in the path lay his beautiful otter-skin quiver. The journey back to camp was a happy one for both White Feather and Singing Colt.

As the friendship between White Feather and Singing Colt grew, so the colt grew. His long legs became swift, and he held his head very high and proudly. He raced with the other ponies and became swift as the wind. When his mane flew back in the wind he was a beautiful sight. In time he became famous as the winner of all races, and White Feather loved him for his beauty and pride.

XIII

THE WOMAN WHO KILLED
THE OWL

No people ever loved their country or enjoyed it more than the Sioux. They loved the beautiful streams by which they camped, and the trees that shaded them and their tipis. They loved the green stretches of plains with its gardens here and there of golden sunflowers over which hovered and played myriads of yellow-winged birds. Moving day was just like traveling from one nice home to another.

One evening a hunting party of several families had camped and were enjoying an evening meal. The buffalo had been plentiful. Much meat had been hung up to dry and the women were tanning the hides for winter garments. Between two stones a fire burned with the coal-like glow of cotton-wood bark. Across these stones lay a large buffalo bone, the meat on which cooked slowly. Every few minutes a woman would turn it over so that it would cook evenly and thoroughly. When it was done, they would crack the bone and eat the marrow, which was brown and tasty.

Soon the meal was done and all gathered about to eat and talk over the adventures of the day. Darkness followed dusk, and the thick-branched trees made it all the darker around the tipi. The air was sweet with fragrance from the wild-rose thickets.

Some owl near-by made his presence known by a hoot every minute or so. He was joined by another, when the hoots came oftener and closer. The Sioux never considered the owl a bird of evil omen, but were fond of the feathers and used them to decorate head-dresses. So no one minded the hooting until it came close to the tipi.

The meal continued until nothing was left of the roast but the bone. Bolder and bolder became the owl. At last the woman, becoming annoyed at the boldness of the owl, picked up the bone and threw it in the direction of the noise. She threw it hard and swift, and all became quiet. No more hooting disturbed the night.

The next morning the hunters were up bright and early. One of them searching for the feathers of the owl was surprised to find the body of an enemy Crow, his temple pierced with the sharp point of the bone. He had imitated the cry of the owl so exactly that he had deceived the Sioux. But he had paid with his life for his rashness in venturing too close to the tipi of the Sioux woman.

XIV

GRANDMOTHER AND THE BEAR

IT WAS August. The wild turnips were growing on the hillsides and the chokecherries were ripe in the thickets along the river.

Grandmother was then a young woman. One day she and some of the girls of the village gathered a number of children and all went up the hillsides to dig for wild turnips, of which the Sioux were very fond. The girls carried long, sharp sticks to pry the turnips from the ground. Grandmother, however, carried an iron rod, for in her day white people were among the Sioux and had brought iron things that the Indians had never before owned.

When a bunch of four or five turnips had been gathered, the long white roots were braided together in order that they could be more easily carried while others were being gathered. When

they were taken home they were hung in the
sun to dry, then put away in rawhide bags where
they would last for a long time. In the winter
the dried turnips were put in the meat soup and
cooked.

The afternoon became very warm and the turnip-
gatherers looked toward the shade of the river
at the foot of the hills. So down the hills they
started, each carrying her bunches of turnips.
Little ones and big ones all carried what they
could, according to their size. When they came
to the river they drank and rested in the shade
of the cottonwoods. Then they wandered through
the cherry bushes, eating what they wanted.

Suddenly everyone was startled by some of
the children running toward Grandmother and
the larger girls, screaming and shouting in terror.
'A bear! A bear!' they screamed. Grandmother
called to all the children to run as fast as possible for home. The bear could now be plainly
heard growling and crashing in the undergrowth.
When the children had all started for home,
Grandmother ran too. But the bear gained on

her. Still shouting to the children not to stop running, she turned around and saw that the bear was very close to her. She ran as fast as she could, but soon realized that she could never outrun the animal. She must do something. Turning suddenly, she pointed the long iron bar straight at the bear, as a hunter would point a gun. To her surprise the bear stopped, though he still growled. Grandmother, seeing the bear's fright, held the bar aimed at him, and to her great relief he turned around in the path and fled out of sight, running as fast as before, only in the opposite direction.

Possibly this bear had once been wounded with the white man's gun, or perhaps he disliked the flash of fire and the smell of powder, or even the roar of the shot.

Whatever it might be, Grandmother was a heroine, and like other heroines was praised for her bravery. Grandmother still lives in the memory of the Sioux people.

XV

THE FAITHFUL HORSE

THE Sioux had returned victorious from a war excursion, and the village was preparing a feast and victory dance for them. Everyone was happy and excited. There was no enemy within many miles, and the territory of the Sioux was free from any who might steal their horses or chase away the buffalo.

The women were busy cooking for the feast and the men were putting on their beautiful feather head-dresses. Those who had received wounds in battle painted themselves red to mark the place of injury. There was much display of painted quivers, lances decorated with strips of otter-skin, fans and banners. Everywhere feathers fluttered in the air. Even the horses which had returned with the men from war were being combed and sweetgrass wreaths placed about their necks. Their tails were braided and decorated with waving fluffs of eagle feathers. They also were painted red if they had been wounded in battle. Every man was proud and fond of the horse that had been with him through battle, and it seemed as if the horses were aware of the unusual attention that was being given them, for they danced and pranced to the sound of the tomtom and the songs of the warriors.

The girls were pretty in soft deerskin dresses and in moccasins and leggings as white as snow. Their long, black, shiny braids were tied with ornaments made from dyed porcupine-quills strung on dyed deerskin strings. At the end of these hair strings there were tassels of bright-colored feathers. Some of them wore the head-dress and robes of the warriors and danced and sang for the brave ones.

In all this gladness one young man was sad. While other young men rode about proudly on their war horses, he was thinking of his own horse which he had left lying dead on the battle-field. The fight had been a heavy one. His horse had fallen under him and he had been left afoot

THE ASTONISHMENT OF THE YOUNG WARRIOR... TURNED TO
GLADNESS

and in a dangerous position, but a friend had rescued him. His friend's pony had carried them both home to safety. So the young brave's mind was on the faithful companion that he had last seen lying on the battlefield. Praises would be sung for his faithful horse, but for all that he could not help feeling sad.

The feasting and dancing lasted for several days, or until all the warriors had been praised. Then one by one the visiting bands had packed their tipis and gone back to their own villages.

Once again all was quiet and the warriors were feeling proud of the honors that had been given them. Evening was coming and everybody was peacefully enjoying the close of a pleasant day. All at once, coming slowly toward the village, was seen the gaunt figure of a horse. He walked slowly but steadily. His head drooped, but he walked straight through the village. Everyone watched, but no one spoke. Across the circle of tipis the pony walked until he reached the one farthest from the side of the circle where he had entered. There he stopped. The astonishment of the young warrior standing by the tipi door turned to gladness, for this thin, tired pony was the one he had been mourning for dead on the battlefield. He stroked the faithful animal's head, patted his back, and touched gently the terrible wound that still gaped red in his side.

As friends gathered about, the wonderful story was again told of the battle and the return of the faithful horse.

XVI

THE MAGIC TREE

A PARTY of Sioux were once on the way to join another band. In the evening camp was made by the edge of a river which ran through a great open grassy plain.

Preparations were made for spending a restful night. One of the mares was staked out and the other animals stayed close by eating the grass which grew in abundance. The moon came up, and the night was nearly as light as day. Objects could be seen almost as if the sun were shining, for the great plain was treeless.

During the night the party was aroused from deep sleep by a crashing and breaking of limbs as if giant trees were being tossed about. The roar was terrifying, and the horses stamped and trembled with fear while the tethered one ran round and round the stake, winding itself close.

The poor beasts strained their eyes to see, and their ears stood forward as they tried to comprehend the awful sounds.

The braves leaped up and grasped their weapons ready to mount their horses. Looking over the plain they were amazed to see an immense cottonwood tree bounding over the ground as if driven by a strong wind, though not even a gentle breeze blew. From the north of the plain it went with crashing and breaking limbs toward the south and out of sight. The braves looked with speechless astonishment as the tree turned over and over in its mad flight. It filled them with wonder, even though they knew that all things are possible to the Great Mystery, which lives and works through all things.

The next morning, as the braves continued their journey, they came upon the path of the tree. Straight across the plain its course was marked with branches and leaves scattered along the way. The Sioux followed the path, which led to a creek, and there they found the tree. It stood straight and leafless, with broken limbs hanging from its trunk. But its roots had already grasped at the soil. The braves knew that the tree had journeyed a long way in order that it might be here among other trees of its own kind. Now it was contented.

The strong roots of the cottonwood went deep into the earth and the branches began to mend. The limbs became covered with green and silvery buds. Soon it was a beautiful green tree, with leaves that trembled in the breeze and glistened in the sun.

XVII

THE YEAR OF THE BUFFALO

ONE time the Sioux were camped on the banks of Big Water River. The camp was a very large one, stretching from the bank of the river to the foothills. It was winter-time, and snow covered everything in sight. The cottonwoods were without leaves, and many of them had been cut down so that the ponies could eat of their bark. This kept the ponies alive through the winter. They were fond of this food.

The supply of meat had begun to run low, and for many weeks the scouts had looked for buffalo, but none could be found. At last the meat was entirely gone, so the scouts went to the Buffalo medicine-man and asked him to bring the buffalo. The Buffalo medicine-man knew all the secrets of the buffalo and talked with them in his visions.

The medicine-man prepared a tipi with an altar, and on it placed a buffalo skull. Then he told all the people in the village to wear their buffalo blankets and to gather about his tipi. Every man, woman, and child put on his blanket and stood in front of the medicine tipi. They looked like a great herd of buffalo. There all stood in silence, and soon there could be heard the roar of the buffalo coming from the tipi.

Then a girl came out carrying the sacred pipe. She walked around the circle and passed the door of every tipi in the village. Then the Buffalo medicine-man came out, rushing and roaring like a buffalo, and wearing the head-dress and robe of the Buffalo Dreamer. He danced here and there among the crowd, bellowing like the buffalo. As he ran, the people parted to let him pass and to avoid being hit with the horns on his head, which he tossed about like an angry buffalo.

The girl walked slowly around the village and the crowd followed while the medicine-man danced. When all had returned to the tipi from which they had started, the medicine-man entered and the rest of the villagers went home.

The next morning, just as the medicine-man

had prophesied, the buffalo came. The Sioux people have never forgotten this event, and to this day that year is known to them as 'The Year of the Buffalo.'

XVIII

THE HOLY DOG

In olden days the Sioux did not have horses.
They had never even heard of one. Their travois
were dragged along by large dogs, and when
the camp was moved these big dogs served as
pack-animals carrying tipis and household goods,
and dragging the travois. Dogs were indispen-
sable to the Sioux, and they had great numbers
of them.

The Sioux dogs were big shaggy fellows, strong
and intelligent. They had lived with the Sioux
in this country and had been his companion, for
a long, long time.

In those days the Indians lived peaceably with
all animals. Even the buffalo would often wander
into the camp of the Sioux and eat the grass
that grew within the circle of the village. They
would usually come during the night, and when

the Sioux awoke in the morning there would be the buffalo feeding on the green grass. When the smoke began to rise from the tipis and the people began to stir about, the buffalo would move away. It was as if the Great Mystery sent the buffalo, so that if meat were needed it would be there at hand. In fact, many times if there was need for meat, a buffalo could be had for the morning meal. Those were the days of plenty for the Sioux.

One morning the Sioux came out of their tipis and there were the buffalo close by feeding as usual. Soon they moved away, but still feeding around was a strange-looking object such as had never before been seen. It seemed very gentle, not heeding the people, who stared at it curiously. No one ventured near at first, for the animal was too strange, and no one knew its habits. They did not know whether it would bite or kick or run. Everyone stared, but still the animal fed on, scarcely lifting its head to look at those who began to walk closer for a better view. The head of this strange animal

THE HEAD OF THIS STRANGE ANIMAL WAS NOT SHAGGY LIKE THAT
OF THE BUFFALO

was not shaggy like that of the buffalo. Its eyes were large and soft-looking, like those of the deer, and its legs were slender and graceful. A mane flowed from its neck, and its tail reached nearly to the ground. The beauties of this strange animal were greatly praised by first one and then another.

Then some hunter got a rawhide rope. Maybe this animal would permit being tied, for it seemed so gentle. The rope was thrown, but the animal escaped, for it raised its head on its long slender neck and raced around a short distance, not in fright nor in anger, but as if annoyed. How handsome this animal was when it ran! It did not resemble the buffalo, nor deer, nor wolf, but was more beautiful than any of these.

The rope was thrown again and again, and at last it was on the neck of the animal. It seemed only more kind and gentle, and stood tamely while some dared to stroke it gently. Now and then it nibbled at the grass as if aware it was among friends. Admiration for the lovely animal grew. All wanted to stroke its neck and forehead, and the creature seemed at once to enjoy this extra attention. Finally a warrior grew brave enough to mount upon its back. Then all laughed and shouted with joy. What a wonderful creature! It must have come straight from the Great Mystery!

The people did not know that in later years this animal was to come to them in great numbers and was to become as great a friend to them as the dog. Both the hunter and the warrior came in time to think of it as an inseparable companion in peace and in war, for it faithfully shared the work of the long-time friend of the Sioux — the dog.

The Sioux loved their dogs — their daily companions in camp or on the trail. And liking the strange lovely animal so well, they could think of no better name to call it than the Holy Dog.

So to this day the horse to the Sioux is *Sunke Wakan* — 'Holy Dog.'

XIX

THUNDER HORSE

THE Thunder Dreamer knows that in the sky dwell the warriors of Thunder and Lightning, for he has seen and spoken to them in his vision.

These warriors ride wildly about on the black clouds astride their handsome horses, holding in their hands the lightning-sticks which flash during a thunderstorm. Everyone has seen them flash as the warriors dash about in the stormy sky. Whenever the hoofs of the horses boom, the lightning-sticks flash blindingly.

One day the Sioux were all in their tipis waiting for a thunderstorm to pass. The Thunder and Lightning warriors were dashing back and forth across the sky. Their horses ran madly, for the noise from their feet was deafening. Mingled with the noise of trampling hoofs were the frequent flashes from the lightning-sticks. Great drops of rain fell and ran off the sides of the tipis. The women threw cedar leaves on the fire, and everyone huddled closer.

Suddenly the noise increased to one awful roar. Two lightning-sticks came together, for there was a blinding flash of white light. The tipis shook and the people were fear-stricken.

Two warriors had rushed together, and their horses, losing their balance, fell to earth, where they struggled for an instant, then dashed back to the sky. When the storm had cleared, on a great rock close by the village was plainly to be seen the hoofprint of a great horse. It is there to this day for all to see.

XX

THE FIRST FIRE

A Sioux scout, tired and weary from a long journey, sat down on the plain to rest. Beside him lay a fallen yucca plant with its long body stretched upon the ground. The scout aimlessly picked up a small stick that lay near-by, and, rubbing it between his hands upon the yucca, noticed a thin blue vapor arising.

This vapor smelled very pleasant as it rose in the air and disappeared. The scout thought that, since it went up and out of sight, it must go to the land of the Sky People. And going up so far it would, no doubt, carry a message to those who lived in the sky.

So the scout played on, enjoying the blue clouds of smoke as they ascended and disappeared in the air. After a while a small red and orange flame burst from the tip of the stick.

It was beautiful, and the heat that came with it was very agreeable. Interested now beyond all care to continue his journey, the scout watched the stick and yucca plant change into this lovely flame that sprang up, looking like a beautiful plume, only to fade away and form into another just as beautiful. How strange and yet how beautiful it is, thought the scout. He never wanted to lose this beautiful being, whatever it was.

So he fed the flame with more yucca, and it lived and grew. He could not leave it here to perish, and yet he was forced to go home at last. So he carried a burning wand back to the village with him, and in the center, where all could see, he made it grow with more yucca. All the people of the village came and sat about, marveling at the wonder of it all.

This gorgeous red flame was warming to the hands and body, but could hurt severely if one got too close. It looked soft and caressing, but stung the fingers if one tried to catch and hold the lovely curling feathers of fire. The wood which was put in these flames to keep them alive turned into brilliant red coals that sparkled and changed color too. So all day the village people watched, and when evening came they were still gathered there. This marvel was something like the sun, for it lighted up the space in which they sat. Strange it did not do this in the daytime. Only at night. This fascinating being had wondrous ways hard to understand.

Since the beautiful flame burned one's hands and toes, what would it do to meat? A piece of buffalo meat was held close, and as the flames wound about it the odor was strangely tempting. The meat was tasted, and it was good. Everyone tasted the meat that came from the red-hot coals, and all found it delicious. No longer would the Sioux prepare their meat only by the heat of the sun.

And so this is the way fire was brought to the Sioux people. The man who brought it to them is great in their history.

THE END